©Andy & Susan Caffrey

Welsh Recipes

A selection of recipes from around Wales

By **Amanda Wragg**

BRADWELL
BOOKS

Published by Bradwell Books

9 Orgreave Close Sheffield S13 9NP

Email: books@bradwellbooks.co.uk

British Library Cataloguing in Publication Data: a catalogue record for this book is available from the British Library.

1st Edition

ISBN: 9781902674827

Print: Gomer Press, Llandysul, Ceredigion SA44 4JL TBC

Artwork and design by: Andrew Caffrey

Photographic Credits:
  Front Cover: Left-Right
  Shutterstock/paul Cowan
  Shutterstock/Monkey Business Business
  Shutterstock/D. Pimborough
  Shutterstock/Jane Rix

Bottom
  Shutterstock/David Hughes

Back Cover
  Andy & Susan Caffrey

The photographs used in this book are to illustrate the dish and are not meant as a final representation of the finished result. Any garnish or additions are at your discretion.

Recipes

Introduction

Shutterstock/Vepar5

Wales, a beguiling, bewitching part of the world with an incredibly diverse landscape; towering mountains, lush, deep valleys and a dramatic coastline – time spent in this magnificent country will stay in the memory for ever. From the perennially popular family seaside resorts Llandudno and Rhyl in the north to the vibrant, cosmopolitan capital Cardiff in the south, Wales offers something for everyone, including foodies!

Much of Wales' traditional food has travelled all over the world and most of us are familiar with ancient recipes handed down through generations; who hasn't tried a slice of bara brith or tucked into a plate of Welsh rarebit? Cawl is a robust, wholesome stew made with seafood if you're near the coast or with hardy Welsh lamb if you're in the hills — either way it's a delicious dish, guaranteed to warm your cockles. Laverbread — not bread at all but edible seaweed — has been a traditional ingredient for millennia, and these days it's relatively simple to source so we can include it in our recipes.

Craggy slopes and glacial hillsides produce sweet lamb and Black Beef cattle, native to Wales, have deliciously tender, naturally marbled meat — you really will be able to distinguish it if you're eating out. Talking of which, Wales has a smattering of Michelin stars so you won't struggle for top-notch eating experiences if that's your thing. Whilst much of traditional Welsh cooking is honest and hearty, home cooks and award-winning chefs from Gwynedd to Gwent are using a phenomenal range of local ingredients to produce delicious dishes, some of which are reproduced here.

I'm indebted to my good friend Llinos John from Anglesey for sharing some of her family recipes with me, to Bryan Webb at the fabulous Tyddyn Llan restaurant in Llandrillo, Ffiona and Brian Thomas (two of Rick Stein's Food Heroes!) for their Welsh Black Beef winter warmer recipe and Andrew Nutter for his shallot and bacon tart.

Shutterstock/KateChris

Amanda Wragg

Vegetable Stock

Since time immemorial country people the world over have kept the stockpot simmering all day on the kitchen stove. Those days are pretty much gone, but making a good basic stock isn't difficult and although there are many quick options these days (even one or two of our 'top' chefs are advertising stock cubes!) there's nothing as satisfying as knowing your soup, stew or casserole is made with the real deal. This flavoursome stock will last for up to a week in the fridge, or batch freeze it for later use. Many cooks make different stocks depending on what they're the basis of; beef, fish, chicken – but I find this basic stock will do nicely for any dish you're making.

Ingredients

3 medium onions

5 medium carrots

3 medium leeks

3 sticks celery

8 cabbage leaves

Handful flat leaf parsley

3 sprigs fresh thyme

1 bay leaf

Sea salt

3.5 litres cold water

Method

1   Roughly chop the vegetables and put in a large saucepan or stockpot with all the other ingredients.

2   Cover with water and bring slowly to the boil.

3   Reduce the heat to a gentle simmer. Skim off any scum.

4   Simmer very gently with the lid ajar for an hour, skimming from time to time.

5   Strain through a sieve – don't push any of the soft vegetables through as the stock will become cloudy. Allow to cool then refrigerate.

ShutterStock/Ben Smith

Soda Bread

There are many artisan bakers around Wales, but there is nothing quite like filling the house with the smell of home-baked bread. It is much easier than most people think, especially using the soda bread recipe below; you'll get one largish loaf or three smaller ones. Soda bread tends to be denser than yeasted bread, so don't be surprised if it doesn't rise quite as much as you might expect.

Ingredients

400g wholemeal flour

75g plain white flour (you can use strong bread flour if you have it)

1 tsp salt

1 tsp bicarbonate of soda

1 large egg

1 tbsp vegetable oil of your choice

1 tsp honey, treacle or soft brown sugar, whichever you have to hand

425ml buttermilk or sour milk*

*To make sour milk, take 425ml milk, add the juice of ½ a lemon, give it a quick stir, leave for 10 minutes and off you go.

Method

1   Preheat the oven to 400F/200°C/gas 6. Prepare a loaf tin (23 x 12.5 x 5cm) by brushing with vegetable oil or lining with a paper liner, or use smaller tins if you prefer.

2   Put the dry ingredients into a large bowl and sieve in the bicarbonate of soda. Mix well.

3   Whisk the egg and then add the oil, sugar/honey/treacle and the buttermilk or sour milk. Make a well in the centre of the dry ingredients and pour in all the liquid. Using a large wooden spoon mix well, scraping the flour from the sides until all the ingredients are blended into a smooth, slightly gloopy mixture. Add more milk if necessary.

4   Pour into the loaf tin(s) and sprinkle on some seeds on top if you fancy (sunflower seeds or linseeds are nice).

5   Put in the oven for an hour and then check to see if the loaf is cooked through using a skewer. If the bread is ready it will sound hollow when you knock it on the bottom, and the skewer should come out clean.

Shutterstock/Lyudmila Suvarova

9

Omelette

Sometimes the simplest dishes are the best. If you're strapped for time (or cash) a straightforward omelette hits the spot. Some folk are anxious around making them – but don't fear, very little can go wrong! You can ring the changes by adding all sorts: mushrooms, tomatoes or cheese. You'll find fabulous cheeses throughout Wales; on this occasion I recommend award-winning Gorwydd Caerphilly from the Trethowans Dairy in Ceredigion – available to buy all over England and Wales.

Ingredients
SERVES 1

2 large free-range eggs

Sea salt

Freshly ground black pepper

1 small knob of butter

1 small handful of grated farmhouse cheese

Method

1 Crack the eggs into a bowl with a pinch of salt & pepper. Beat well with a fork. Put a small pan on a low heat and add the butter. When it's melted and starting to bubble, add the eggs, moving them round the pan to spread them out evenly.

2 When the eggs start to firm up but still with a bit of raw on top, sprinkle over the cheese. Ease round the edges of the omelette then fold it over, in half. When it starts to turn golden brown underneath, slide it from the pan onto a plate.

3 Snip some parsley, chives or basil over the top and tuck in with a chunk of home made bread and glass of wine.

Shutterstock/Tatiana Frank

Pickled Red Cabbage

This tasty (and easy to make) accompaniment to cheese and meat is also a great idea for a present if you find a pretty jar to put it in. It takes a bit of time but it's worth it. Works brilliantly well with any casserole or stew.

The cabbage is steeped in salt for about 3 hours then boiled for around 40 minutes.

Ingredients

500g red cabbage

140g sea salt

500ml cider vinegar

200ml red wine

400g granulated sugar

2 tsp black peppercorns

6 bay leaves

2 tbsp yellow mustard seeds

2 red chillies sliced very thin

Method

1	Place the shredded cabbage in a colander over the sink and sprinkle with salt. Leave for 2-3 hours, then drain and wash away the salt. Pat dry with a clean tea towel.
2	Put the vinegar, wine, sugar, peppercorns and bay leaves into a big, wide saucepan and simmer until the liquid has reduced by about half – about 40 minutes.
3	Strain through a fine sieve into a jug or bowl, and discard the peppercorns and bay leaves. Put the cabbage and mustard seeds into a big bowl, and then pour the strained liquid over.
4	Transfer the cabbage and pickling liquid into sterilised jars and seal. It will last up to a month in the fridge.

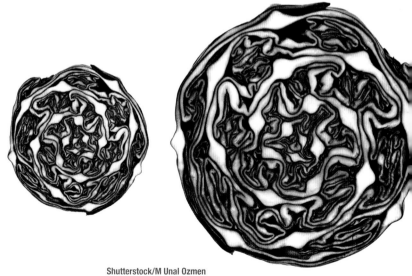

Shutterstock/M Unal Ozmen

Simple Pasta Sauce

Wales has long had a large Italian population and you'll find their influence throughout the country, on menus and in delis. This simple, delicious, tomato-based sauce is great with pasta — all you need add is a grating of parmesan, a sprinkling of basil and a glass of red wine. Perfect after a long day at the office when all you want to do is throw supper together.

Ingredients SERVES 2

Olive oil

1 red onion, finely chopped

4 cloves of garlic, finely chopped

A handful of black olives, stoned and halved

Pinch of chilli flakes

Tin of chopped tomatoes

1 tsp sugar

Sea salt

Freshly ground black pepper

4 basil leaves

Pasta of your choice — literally any will do; spaghetti, penne, linguine or those cute little bow ties

Method

1   Warm a slug of olive oil in a frying pan. Add the chopped onion and garlic
    and cook gently until starting to colour. Add the chilli flakes, sugar, olives and
    the tin of tomatoes. Season to taste.

2   Let it bubble for about 15
    minutes (adding a bit of
    water if it's starting to
    look dry).

3   In the meantime cook
    your pasta in a large pan
    of boiling salted water.
    Drain, put in warm bowls
    and drop the tomato
    sauce on the top. Grate
    parmesan on the top and
    finish with the basil leaves.

©Joan Ransley

Leek & Potato Soup

Nothing says 'Wales' more than leek and potato soup, and this recipe is guaranteed to warm the cockles; on a chilly winter's day it's the perfect lunch or supper. It's simple, cheap to make and freezes really well.

Ingredients

3 leeks

1 white onion

25g butter

500g potatoes

1.5 litres stock (home made - see page 6 or use Marigold Bouillon)

Sea salt

Freshly ground black pepper

Pinch of nutmeg

150ml single cream

Snipped chives to garnish

Method

1   Cut the top and bottom off the leeks and cut in half lengthways, then into fine slices. Rinse in a sink of cold water to get rid of any grit and drain. Peel the onion and slice thinly.

2   Melt the butter in a pan and add the leeks and onion; stir well and cook for about 5 minutes, until the vegetables are soft, making sure you don't brown them.

3   Peel the potatoes and slice them (about ¼ ") and add to the pan when the leeks and onion are soft then add the stock. Add a little salt and pepper – not too much at this point. Add a generous pinch of nutmeg, turn up the heat and bring to the boil. Reduce to a simmer and cook for about 10 minutes or until all the vegetables are soft.

4   Remove from the heat and let it cool a little before blitzing it with a stick blender. Once it's smooth return to the heat and re-warm it gently, adding the cream at the last minute.

5   Ladle into bowls and add the chives as a garnish. Serve with home made soda bread (see page 8).

Shutterstock/Jane Rix

Shallot & Bacon Tart with Rarebit Topping

This simple, tasty tart has a hint of Wales with the rarebit topping. A great dinner party starter, it might seem a bit fiddly, but once you've made it a couple of times you'll find it a doddle. Make your own pastry if you will, but ready-made will do just as well.

My thanks go to chef/owner Andrew Nutter for allowing me to use his recipe. Andrew runs his eponymous restaurant in Lancashire and is a huge fan of Welsh food.

Ingredients SERVES 4

For the rarebit:	For the shallot & bacon mix:
200g Welsh cheese	**3 tbsp** olive oil
100g White Stilton cheese	**6** rashers streaky bacon cut into thin strips
30ml milk	**10** shallots, finely chopped
25g plain flour	**1** garlic clove, finely chopped
25g white breadcrumbs	**2** tbsp honey
3 egg yolks	**2** handfuls of fresh spinach, shredded
2 tbsp Dijon mustard	
1 tbsp Worcestershire Sauce	

Method

For the pastry tarts:

1   Roll about 250g of pastry onto a lightly floured surface then divide between 4 individual tart cases. Prick with a fork then bake blind for about 8 minutes until golden and crisp.

For the rarebit:

1   Put the cheese and milk into a heavy-bottomed pan and heat slowly, stirring all the while, until the cheese melts. Add the flour and breadcrumbs and cook for about a minute, until the cheese thickens and comes away from the edge of the pan.

2   Remove from the heat, cool slightly then put the whole lot in a food processor. Add the egg yolks, mustard and Worcestershire Sauce and blend until smooth.

For the sticky shallot filling:

1   Heat the olive oil in a frying pan and add the bacon until golden. Add the chopped shallots, garlic and honey and cook on a low heat for 5 minutes. Stir in the shredded spinach and season to taste.

2   When ready to serve, divide the shallot mixture into the tartlet cases, reserving some for garnish. Pour the rarebit over the top, ensuring it covers the whole tart. Bake in a hot oven for 5 minutes. Finish off under a hot grill until glazed and golden. Serve with a simple green salad.

Beetroot and Cheese Salad

This is a stunningly robust salad, full of earthiness and sweetness. Any soft cheese will do – but Cothi Valley's goat's cheese is the perfect ingredient. If you choose to cook the beetroot from scratch, allow an hour in the oven (wrap each one in foil), but vacuum-packed cooked beets do the job just as well.

Ingredients SERVES 4

6 medium sized cooked beetroots (room temperature)

250g crumbly cheese

For the dressing

2 tbsp white wine vinegar

½ tsp Dijon mustard

5 tbsp olive oil

1 tsp caraway seeds

Sea salt and freshly ground black pepper

Slices of home made bread to serve (see page 8)

Method

1   Mix together the vinegar, mustard and seasoning. Beat the olive oil in with a whisk, bit by bit. Toast the caraway seeds lightly under the grill then add them to the dressing.

2   Shred the beetroot, add the dressing, crumble the cheese into chunks and scatter through the beets. Serve with thick slices of home made bread.

©Joan Ransley

Caerphilly and Tomato Salad

What could be easier than throwing some cheese and tomatoes together on a plate? Nothing! This simple, delicious recipe is great for a quick supper, as a dinner party starter or a side dish to your main course. It makes the most of Wales' greatest exports, Caerphilly, a hard, white cow's cheese which is delightfully tangy and nutty. Make sure you serve it at room temperature!

Ingredients SERVES 4

175g Caerphilly cheese

4 medium vine tomatoes

1 tbsp olive oil

150g natural yoghurt

½ tsp English mustard

2 tbsp freshly chopped herbs (choose from chives, parsley, chervil or marjoram)

Sea salt

Freshly ground black pepper

Method

1 Slice the tomatoes and crumble the cheese onto a pretty plate. Whisk all the other ingredients together in a small bowl, then season.

2 Spoon the dressing over the cheese and tomato, sprinkle with flat leaf parsley and serve with chunks of warm home made bread (see page 8).

Shutterstock/margouillat photo

Welsh Cheese and Thyme Tarts

These tasty tarts are simple to make and easy on the purse. Eat them warm or cold – either way you can't fail to impress the family or dinner guests. Classic Welsh Caerphilly will do nicely here - or if you can get hold of Acorn, use that. It's a modern farmhouse artisan cheese made from unpasteurized ewe's milk, and has a wonderful texture – firm and crumbly at the same time – perfect for vegetarians too.

Ingredients SERVES 4

Packet ready-made short crust pastry

1 onion, thinly sliced

1 red pepper, thinly sliced

150g Caerphilly cheese

120ml double cream

1 medium egg

1 sprig thyme, leaves removed and finely chopped

Sea salt and freshly ground black pepper

Method

1. Pre-heat the oven to 375F/190C/gas 5. Roll out the pastry to the thickness of a pound coin on a lightly floured surface. Line the pastry cases then top with a disk of greaseproof paper and baking beans. Cook for 10 minutes.

2. Remove the paper and beans and cook for a further 5 minutes. Remove and leave to cool.

To make the filling:

3. Gently fry the onion and red pepper in a tablespoon of olive oil until they're soft but not brown. Divide between the four cases. Crumble the cheese on top of the onions.

4. Whisk the cream and egg together, add the thyme, season and pour into the cases.

5. Cook in the middle of the oven for 15 minutes (the pastry will be a lovely golden brown and the cheese mix bubbling). Serve hot or cold with a green salad and a fat slice of brown bread.

©Joan Ransley

Fish Parcels

There's a long history of coastal and inland fishing in Wales, and it's not difficult to source sustainable fish of all kinds throughout the country. This simple but incredibly tasty dish works well with firm white fish, though it works well with salmon too.

Ingredients

1 fillet of fish per portion (you could use salmon, cod or haddock)

A couple of lemon slices (optional)

Fish stock

Fresh dill or oregano (you get a better result with fresh, but you can use always use dried instead)

Baking parchment or aluminium foil

Sea salt

Freshly ground black pepper

Caerphilly cheese, grated

Method

1   Pre-heat your oven to 180C/gas 4. Prepare pieces of foil or baking
    parchment big to make a reasonable sized parcel for each fillet of fish.

2   Place the fish in the middle of the foil or parchment and form up the sides of
    the parcel. If using lemon slices, place them under the fish fillet. Sprinkle with
    a little fish stock, seasoning and some herbs.

3   Close up your parcel, being careful not to lose your stock. Place in the
    pre-heated oven on a baking tray. Bake for around 10 minutes; the exact
    cooking time will depend on the fish and its thickness.

4   When the fish is cooked, remove from the parcel, sprinkle with a handful
    of grated Lancashire cheese and grill until melted and golden. Serve with a
    salad garnish as a starter, or accompanied by salad and boiled new potatoes
    as a main course.

Christopher Elwell/Shutterstock

Welsh Cawl

Cawl is a deeply traditional stew and has been dished up on farmhouse tables for centuries; if you are inland or on the hills it's made with lamb or mutton, by the coast it will be brimming with seafood. This robust, hearty recipe requires lamb. Some people like to add lentils or pearl barley in the depths of winter – I certainly do.

Ingredients SERVES 6

6 small Welsh lamb shanks

1 ltr home made stock - see page 6 - or use Marigold Bouillon

225g potatoes, peeled & diced

225g swede, peeled & diced

225g onions, peeled & chopped

225g carrots, peeled & diced

225g leeks, cleaned and sliced thin

A bunch of herbs: bay, thyme, rosemary & parsley

a small Savoy cabbage, shredded

2 tbsp vegetable oil

Sea salt

Freshly ground black pepper

Method

1   Heat the vegetable oil in a large pan, season the lamb shanks and put in
    the pan with the onion and brown all over – you may have to do this in
    batches if the pan's not large enough. Pour the stock in and add the herbs.
    Season well. Bring to the
    boil then reduce the heat
    to a simmer. Cover and
    cook for 40 minutes.

2   Add all the other
    vegetables except for the
    cabbage and cook for a
    further 30 minutes. Add
    the shredded cabbage
    and cook for a further
    10 minutes.

3   Top the stock up if it
    reduces, or add a glass
    of red wine. Serve with
    mashed potatoes.

Shutterstock/Monkey Business Images

Welsh Lamb Shepherds Pie

Cottage pie (made with beef) or Shepherd's pie (made with lamb) are the kings of comfort food, can be made a day in advance (tastes even better) and represents great value for money! Welsh lamb is particularly sweet and flavoursome.

Ingredients SERVES 4

Vegetable oil

100g lamb mince

1 large onion, finely chopped

1 carrot, finely chopped

2 celery sticks, finely chopped

Clove garlic, finely chopped

6 mushrooms, sliced

1 sprig thyme

200ml stock (Marigold is the best, but any good stock cube will do)

Worcestershire Sauce

1 tin chopped tomatoes

450g potatoes

Knob of butter

Salt

Freshly ground black pepper

Handful of grated farmhouse cheese

Method

1   Heat a tablespoon of oil in a large pan and gently brown the mince. Remove
     and add the chopped vegetables to the pan. Cook for about five minutes or
     until they've softened a bit.

2   Add the mince, a good dash of relish, the tomatoes, stock, thyme and
     season generously with salt & pepper. Let it bubble away for about an hour,
     until the stock has reduced by half.

3   In the meantime, peel the potatoes, cut them into small-ish chunks, put in
     cold water with a pinch of salt and bring to the boil. Let them simmer away
     for about 20 minutes, until
     they're soft.

4   Drain, add a knob of butter,
     a splash of milk, and mash.
     Put the mince mixture into an
     ovenproof dish, cover with the
     mashed potatoes, sprinkled
     on the cheese and put in a
     medium hot oven for about 15
     minutes until the cheese has
     browned up. Serve with minted
     peas and pickled red cabbage
     (see page 12).

Shutterstock/violeta pasat

Roast Wild Bass with Laverbread butter Sauce

A modern twist on a Welsh classic, this recipe comes from chef Bryan Webb at Tyddyn Llan in Clwyd, to whom I am greatly indebted. Laverbread is a traditional ingredient – it's actually edible seaweed and at one time was quite hard to source, but now often available in many supermarkets. Whilst it might appear a bit time-consuming, it's quite simple, and guaranteed to impress at any dinner party.

Ingredients SERVES 4

4 x 150g pieces of wild bass, skin on and all pin bones removed

4 finely chopped shallots

1 tablespoon of white wine vinegar

175ml dry white wine

250g unsalted butter

Salt and a pinch of cayenne pepper

Juice of half a lemon

2 tablespoon of laverbread

2 tablespoon of double cream

300g raw spinach

50g extra butter

Method

For the beurre blanc.

1. Put the white wine, vinegar and shallots into a saucepan and slowly reduce to a syrup.

2. On a light heat slowly add the butter a little at a time until it forms a slightly thick sauce, season with salt and cayenne pepper, add the juice of the half lemon.

3. Strain the sauce into a clean saucepan. In a separate saucepan add two tablespoons of laverbread with 2 tablespoons of cream, bring to the boil and add half the beurre blanc.

4. Season the fish and coat lightly with olive oil place onto a hot griddle skin side down, until the skin is crisp, place onto an oiled tray and bake in a hot oven 200C for five minutes.

5. While the fish is cooking, in a large pan melt the extra butter and cook the spinach until wilted.

6. Serve the bass on a bed of spinach and pour the laverbread sauce around one side and the remaining beurre blanc around the other side.

©Joan Ransley

Lobscouse (Lobscows)

I'm indebted to one of my oldest friends, Llinos, who was born in Llanfaethlu on Anglesey and reports that this dish was one of her family's staples – her mum made it with beef shin and marrow bones. A classic hearty stew, it adorned many a Welsh farmhouse table down the ages and is just as rewarding today. It's cooked slowly, and like many stews tastes even better the following day. The name has its origins in Norway (where it's Lapskaus) and of course in Liverpool it's known as Scouse. The name came to Wales by way of its major ports; during the 19th century North Wales was the world centre for slate and copper.

Ingredients SERVES 6

1.5kg beef shin

2 marrow bones

6 large potatoes, peeled and cut into large pieces

½ swede, peeled and cut into pieces

1 onion, chopped

4 carrots, peeled and sliced into large pieces

3 leeks, cleaned* and sliced thickly

Sea salt

Freshly ground black pepper

Method

1   Put the meat and bones in a large pan of water and bring to the boil. Cook for around 15 minutes then add the vegetables (except the potatoes). Boil for about 40 minutes, or until the meat is tender.

2   Add the potatoes and continue boiling for another 25 minutes, until the potatoes are tender. Season to taste.

3   It's as simple as that! Serve in large dishes with a large bowl of pickled red cabbage (see page 12) on the side.

*to get grit out of leeks, soak them in a bowl of cold salted water once you've sliced them. Leave for about 10 minutes then drain them; any soil or grit will be left behind.

Shutterstock/travellight

Winter Warmer Stew

Those nice people Brian and Ffiona Thomas from Welsh Black Beef Direct (one of Rick Steins's food heroes) have kindly allowed me to reproduce this delicious, rib-sticking recipe, made by Grandma and consumed by generations of her family. She says it feeds '4 very hungry people'. I serve this with either herb dumplings or mashed spuds. As is the rule with stews, the longer you can keep it in the oven, the better it will taste. If you happen to be in Beaumaris on Anglesey it's worth dropping into their shop on Castle Street – they've a lovely restaurant too.

Ingredients

6 thick sausages (whatever variety you want), chopped into bite-sized chunks

2 large white onions, peeled and roughly chopped

2 peppers (green or red), topped, de-seeded and roughly chopped

2 large courgettes, topped, tailed and roughly chopped

2 tins tomatoes or **1kg** fresh tomatoes

2 garlic cloves

Fresh herbs – thyme, rosemary, basil
(or whatever you have in the garden or can get hold of)

Vegetable stock

Freshly ground black pepper

Method

1   Heat the oil in a frying pan and seal the meat on all sides. Add the onions and garlic and fry gently until golden brown.

2   Transfer the steak and onions to a casserole dish. Add the tomato puree, carrots and herbs. Finally add the stock and season to taste. Bring to the boil on the hob then transfer to a medium oven for about 3 hours.

Ingredients

For the dumplings

75g self raising flour

40g Atora suet

Sea salt

Freshly ground black pepper

1 tbsp chopped parsley

1 tbsp water

Put the flour, suet and parsley in a bowl. Season well with salt & pepper. Stir in enough cold water to make a soft dough, then shape with floured hands into 8 balls. Uncover the casserole, pop the dumpling balls on top and leave the lid off. Cook for a further 20 minutes until the dumplings have risen.

Shutterstock/Paul Cowan

Welsh Cakes
(Pice ar y maen)

A tea time treat which has been passed down through generations of Welsh families, and of course they're as delicious today as they ever were. You might want to double the quantities and make twice as many, since the first batch will be wolfed down. Traditionally they were cooked on a bakestone, but you can use a heavy iron griddle or thick-bottomed frying pan.

Ingredients

225g plain flour

100g Welsh salted butter

75g caster sugar

50g currants

½ tsp baking powder

¼ tsp mixed spice

1 egg, lightly beaten

Pinch of salt

Splash of milk to bind

Caster sugar

Method

1   Sift the dry ingredients together in a bowl. Cut the butter up and rub into the mix. Stir in the sugar and fruit. Stir in the egg and a splash of milk to form a dough.

2   Roll the dough out onto a floured surface to about the thickness of a pound coin. Use a cookie cutter to make rounds. Grease your griddle or frying pan and cook the cakes in batches – they'll only need about 10 minutes, until they're golden brown – keep a close eye on them, they burn quite easily.

3   Let them cool slightly before sprinkling a bit of caster sugar on them. Sit down with the paper and a cup of tea and enjoy the moment before the hoards descend and finish the lot off.

Shutterstock/Paul Cowan

Leek & Cheese Muffins

These delicious, easy to make muffins are a fabulous accompaniment to home made soup (see page 16). Alternatively, just slather a bit of butter on and have them for lunch. It's a win-win situation. Any mature cheddar will do – there are many varieties of Welsh cheese to choose from – I suggest Little Black Bomber from Snowdonia on this occasion.

Ingredients

75g plain flour

1tsp baking powder

¼ tsp bicarbonate of soda

Sea salt

Freshly ground black pepper

50ml milk

1 egg, lightly beaten

100ml vegetable oil

1 leek, finely chopped

Knob of butter

75g mature cheddar, finely grated

Method

1   Preheat the oven to 180C/gas4. Line a muffin tin with 9 cases. Mix all the dry ingredients together then gently stir in the egg, milk and oil.

2   Melt the butter in a small pan and gently soften the leeks – they don't need to be brown, just soft.

3   Gently fold in the cooked leeks and cheese. Spoon the mixture into the muffin cases and place in the oven. Bake for about 25 minutes then test one with a skewer – if it comes out clean, they're done. If not, leave for a further 5 minutes.

Shutterstock/Elena Veselova

Bara Brith

This rich fruit loaf made with tea is produced all over Wales, and is delicious spread with salted Welsh butter. Bara Brith means 'speckled bread' and one version of it is made with yeast rather than flour. Whichever way you choose to look at it, it's a firm family favourite, and will keep for about 10 days in an airtight tin if it hasn't disappeared in one sitting.

Ingredients

450g self raising flour

1 tsp mixed spice

175g soft brown sugar

1 free range egg

1 tbsp orange zest

2 tbsp orange juice

1 tbsp runny honey

300ml cold black tea

450g mixed dried fruit

Honey for glazing

Method

1. Put the dried fruit into a large bowl; pour over the tea, cover and leave to soak overnight. The next day, mix together the sugar, lightly beaten egg, orange juice, zest and honey. Add to the fruit.

2. Sift in the flour and spice, mixing well. Pour the mixture into a buttered loaf tin.

3. Bake in a preheated oven at 160C/gas 3 for about 1 ½ hours. The loaf should be golden in colour and firm to the touch. It's a good idea to check with a skewer – it should come out clean when inserted into the middle. Remove the cake and put on a rack to cool, but not before basting with some warm honey while it's still warm.

Shutterstock/D. Pimborough

Katt Pie

Is it a sweet or savoury pie? It's both! A deeply traditional Welsh dish, Katt pies were sold at fairs in Pembrokeshire. They were originally made individually, but you might want to make one big one for the hungry hoards round the table. Make your own pastry by all means, but no one's going to scold you if you use ready made. No felines were harmed in the making of this recipe.

Ingredients

500g short crust pastry*

225g minced mutton or lamb

225g dried fruit — currants, raisins or sultanas or a mix of all three

225g soft brown sugar

Sea salt

Freshly ground black pepper

Method

1	Preheat the oven to 220C/gas 7. Grease a 25cm/10" pie dish.
2	Roll the pastry out on a floured surface, about the thickness of a pound coin. Line the pie dish with the pastry then layer the filling – the mince, dried fruit, sugar and seasoning. Put a lid on the pie. Slit the top to allow the steam to escape.
3	Bake for about 30 minutes until the pastry is golden brown.

Ingredients

*To make your own pastry

125g plain flour

Pinch of salt

55g butter, cubed

40ml cold water

Put the flour and salt in a large bowl and add the cubes of butter. Use your fingertips to rub the butter into the flour until you have a mixture that resembles coarse breadcrumbs – make sure you've no big lumps of butter left. Try to work quickly so that it doesn't become greasy.

Using a knife, stir in just enough of the cold water to bind the dough together. Wrap the dough in clingfilm and chill for 10 minutes before using. Once chilled, roll out on a lightly floured work top to the required size for your pie or pasty. Job done!

Aberffraw Shortbread (Cacennau Iago)

Aberffraw is a tiny fishing village on the west coast of Anglesey, near the pretty resort of Rhosneigr. These easy to make, delicious biscuits are shell-shaped and for decades have been a feature at Anglesey's yearly show. They last around 10 minutes in this house.

Ingredients

75g plain flour

50g unsalted butter

25g caster sugar

Method

1   Preheat the oven to 220C/gas 7. Beat the sugar into the softened butter. Add a little flour at a time.

2   Roll the dough on a floured surface and stamp into round with a plain cutter, keeping them as thin as possible. The locals mark each circle with a scallop shell and trim them.

3   Put onto a baking sheet and into the oven for around 10 minutes – watch carefully or they'll burn. Sprinkle with sugar while they're still warm.

Shutterstock/Dream79

Welsh Bread & Butter Pudding

A nursery tea time classic, this economical, delicious pudding will put a smile on every face round the table, and is a great way to use up any stale Bara Brith (see page 38) which, though it lasts quite a while will eventually dry up. Bread's fine to use too of course. A good pud will have a proper 'jiggle'! Serve with crème fraiche or clotted cream.

Ingredients SERVES 4

8 slices of stale Bara Brith (see page 38) or medium sliced white bread, crusts off

75g unsalted butter

60g sultanas

Grated zest of a lemon

220ml full fat milk

50g caster sugar

2 medium eggs

Vanilla essence

Method

1   Preheat the oven at 190c/gas 5. Butter the Bara Brith or bread. Cut into squares and put into a buttered dish, layering the bread with the sultanas and lemon zest.

2   Beat the eggs with half the sugar and add the milk and vanilla essence. Pour this custard over the bread mix and sprinkle the remaining sugar on and some raisins on top.

3   Cook on the middle shelf of the oven for 30 minutes or until the top is golden brown. Cool to just above room temperature before serving.

Shutterstock/Jamie Rogers

Anglesey Eggs

This simple but luxurious recipe has its roots in an Easter custom on Anglesey which is still adhered to: children go round chanting **'clap clap gofyn wy, I hogia' bach ar y plwy'** or **'clap, clap, ask for an egg for little boys in the parish'**. Who knows what they did with it – but I do know that this tea time treat goes down a storm with all ages.

Ingredients

800g potatoes, peeled and diced

3 tbsp milk

600g leeks, cleaned (see page 31) and finely chopped

25g butter

4 eggs, soft boiled

Sea salt

Freshly ground black pepper

For the cheese sauce:

25g butter

25g cornflour

300g milk

75g Caerphilly cheese

Seasoning

Method

1   Bring the potatoes to boil in salted water. When they're soft, drain and mash with warm milk and add a pinch of salt and a grinding of black pepper. In the meantime, melt the butter in a large pan and add the leeks – don't let them brown, just gently cook them until they're translucent. Add them to the mashed potatoes and fold them through gently.

2   Spoon the mixture into 4 gratin dishes and make a hollow in the centre of each one. Shell the eggs and cut them in half, placing each half yolk side down in the hollow of each dish.

For the cheese sauce:

1   Melt the butter in a saucepan. When it's bubbling gently add the cornflour and make a roux. Slowly add the milk, stirring all the while. When the sauce has thickened, take it off the heat and add the grated cheese, salt & pepper. Return to the heat and keep stirring as the cheese melts.

2   Spoon the sauce over the eggs and sprinkle the remaining cheese over the top. Place the dishes under a medium hot grill until they're warmed through and the cheese has browned nicely.

3   Serve with a simple green salad dressed with lemon juice and a sprinkling of white wine vinegar.

©Joan Ransley

Crispy potato cake

This is a version of Dauphinoise potatoes; in Wales it's served traditionally on St David's Day. In this house it's served all year round as a side dish, often with poached fish, or a main supper dish. The crisp, golden, glazed spuds are irresistible – I've never had to warm them up the next night, they just disappear...

Ingredients

1.5kg medium roasting potatoes – King Edwards or Maris Pipers work well here

3 oz butter, melted

1 tbsp thyme leaves and 1 sprig

2 tbsp olive oil

Sea salt

Method

1   Heat oven to 220C/gas 7. Peel the potatoes and place them in a pan of cold, salted water. Bring to the boil, simmer for 3 minutes and drain. When cool enough to handle, slice a few very neatly.

2   Coat the bottom of a round, ovenproof, non-stick pan with butter then place a sprig of thyme in the middle. Cover with a slice of potato in the middle then arrange the rest of the slices over the base of the pan, overlapping the slices in concentric circles. Slice the rest of the potatoes and tip into a bowl. Pour over the rest of the butter, the nutmeg and the thyme leaves and season with salt and pepper. Toss everything together then tip the seasoned potatoes over the arranged slices and press down gently to flatten.

3   The potato cake can be prepared up to a day ahead and kept covered in the fridge.

4   Cook the cake in the oven below the beef. Every now and then, remove it, press it down with a spatula and drizzle the surface with a little olive oil. Cook for an hour or just over, until the sides look brown and crispy. Carefully invert the cake onto a serving dish or board, scatter with sea salt and serve cut into wedges.

Shutterstock/Timolina

Black Beef Burger

The Welsh Black is a native breed and the meat is renowned for its deep flavour due mainly to natural marbling. Everyone has their favourite way of making burgers; I've added beaten egg and breadcrumbs at different times in an effort to bind the ingredients, but in the end I've invariably opted for the simple approach, which seems to work nicely. The ginger and cumin are optional but give the burger a piquant kick.

Ingredients

1 tbsp oil or butter

1 large onion, finely chopped

1kg roughly minced Black beef steak (or any non-lean mince)

Knob of fresh ginger, grated

1 tsp ground cumin

1 tsp chilli flakes

2 tsp chopped herbs (parsley or thyme work well)

1 tsp salt

Black pepper

Garnishes, sauces and rolls, as desired

Method

1   Heat the oil in a frying pan over a low heat, and cook the onion until soft and slightly browned. Leave to cool.

2   Spread the beef out and sprinkle over the onion. Add the stout, breadcrumbs, herbs and seasoning and mix together with a fork, being careful not to overwork it.

3   Divide the meat into 12 flattish burgers (top tip, wet your hands to stop the meat from sticking) putting a dimple in the centre of each. Cover and refrigerate for an hour.

4   Cook the burgers on a medium to hot barbecue or griddle pan: leave them undisturbed for the first 3 minutes so they build up a good seal on the bottom, then carefully turn them over, adding a slice of cheese on top if desired. Cook for a further 4 minutes for rare, and 7 for well done, and allow to rest for a few minutes before serving. (You can toast buns, cut-side down, on the barbecue at this point).

Shutterstock/Isabelle-Anne Tasse

Welsh Rarebit

There are as many recipes for this wholesome tea time favourite as there are ways to serve it. Author of 'The Art of Cookery' (pub 1747) doyenne Mrs Glasse gives recipes for Scotch, Welch and English rabbit'; the jury's out as to whether or not rabbit is a good addition today!

Ingredients

Slices of good bread: sourdough is best, though home made soda bread (see page 8) works too

200g strong Welsh cheese, grated

1 tsp Dijon mustard

2 spring onions, finely chopped

2 eggs

1 tbsp flour

Method

1   Mix the cheese, mustard, spring onions together with the egg yolk. Whisk briskly and add the flour, whisk again.

2   In a separate bowl, whish the eggs whites until they form soft peaks. Gently fold the whites into the cheese mix.

3   In the meantime, toast the slices of bread. Spread the mixture on the toast and put back under the grill until bubbling and golden.

4   Serve with a simple salad dressed with lemon juice.

©Joan Ransley

Glamorgan Sausages

This delicious dish is ideal for the vegetarians in your life – they take a small amount of preparation and patience, but are simple enough to make and they're an impressive supper dish or dinner party starter.

Ingredients

225g fresh white breadcrumbs

125g grated Caerphilly cheese

3 free range eggs

A splash of milk

Sea salt

Freshly ground black pepper

½ tsp English mustard powder

1 small leek, shredded finely

Knob of butter

Handful of chopped parsley

For the coating:

100g fresh white breadcrumbs

Sea salt

Freshly ground black pepper

1 free range egg

4 tbsp milk

Vegetable oil for frying

Method

1   Put the breadcrumbs, cheese, seasoning, mustard, leek and parsley into a mixing bowl and combine thoroughly. Beat the eggs lightly and add to the ingredients then mix to form a firm dough; you may need a splash of milk if the mixture is a little dry. Divide into 16, and form each portion into a sausage shape. (Top tip: wet your hands for this – you'll find you're able to mould the shapes more easily!)

2   For the coating, beat the egg and add the milk. Put the breadcrumbs on a plate and season generously. Take each sausage and roll it in the egg mixture then roll in the breadcrumbs. Repeat until all the sausages are coated then chill for 30 minutes.

3   Heat a tablespoon of olive oil in a heavy based frying pan then add the sausages and cook over a medium-low heat until golden all over. The sausages should fry gently; if the heat is too high they will brown too quickly and not be cooked through.

4   These sausages go nicely with a tomato salad. Use ripe vine tomatoes, sliced together with a little red onion very thinly sliced. Make a dressing with olive oil, balsamic vinegar, sea salt and freshly ground black pepper.

©Joan Ransley

Melty Onion Toasts

This simple recipe is great for a snack or supper (depending on how hungry you are) or a rather cool dinner party starter. The slug of brandy elevates a fairly ordinary dish into something you'd pay strong money for in a gastropub. Lancych mature, sweet cheese from the fabulous Caws Cenarth farm in Carmarthenshire works beautifully here, but you can use any farmhouse cheddar.

Ingredients

50g butter

6 white onions, finely sliced

2 tsp golden caster sugar

6 slices sourdough or soda bread (see page 8)

300g cheese, crumbled

Watercress and your fave dressing

Method

1   Heat the butter in a medium sized, thick-bottomed frying pan. Add the onions then sprinkle the sugar over. Sweat the onions for about 20 minutes over a medium heat, stirring occasionally, until golden and sticky. Add the brandy and reduce it to almost nothing. Season generously. *You can make this a couple of days in advance – keep it covered in the fridge.

2   Heat the oven to 180C/gas 6. Toast the bread, spread the onions over then top with crumbled cheese. Place on a baking try then pop in the oven for about 15 minutes until bubbling and golden.

3   Serve each piece on a plate with a sprig of watercress.

©Joan Ransley

Tatw Pum Munud
(Five Minute Potatoes)

Another simple, delicious, deeply traditional recipe supplied by my Welsh friend Llinos. Despite its name it takes half an hour or so to cook! Llinos's mum made the stock from the Sunday carcass – nothing was wasted – and they'd tuck in on a Monday tea time after school.

Ingredients SERVES 4

8 potatoes (Maris Piper, Roosters or King Edwards work well) peeled and thinly sliced

1 white onion, thinly sliced

8 rashers smoked back bacon, diced (use the best you can)

300ml stock (home made - see page 6) or use Marigold Bouillon

Method

1. Fry the bacon in a thick bottomed pan until it's golden and starting to frazzle round the edges. Remove from the pan, leaving the fat behind. Add the onions and soften them for a few minutes.

2. Add the sliced potatoes and plenty of black pepper (no salt required!) and mix through, then scatter the bacon over the top. Add the stock until it comes just below the bacon. Put the lid on the pan and simmer for about 25 minutes or until the potatoes are cooked and most of the liquid is gone.

©Joan Ransley

Store Cupboard Staples

Worcestershire Sauce
Gourmet Garden Herbs
& Spices (ginger, garlic,
coriander, basil, chilli,
thai spices)
Marigold Swiss
Vegetable Bouillon
Kallo stock cubes
Instant yeast
Dried thyme
Olive oil
Vegetable oil
Bay leaves
Block of parmesan
Tinned chopped tomatoes
English mustard
Dijon mustard

Wholegrain mustard
Ground cumin
Ground coriander
Ground cinnamon
Ground mace
Ground cloves
Ground ginger
Mixed spice
Raisins
Currants
Pearl barley
Jar of pitted black olives
Chilli flakes
Black peppercorns
Sea salt (Maldon is the
best, but any will do)

Ready made short crust
pastry
Golden syrup
White wine vinegar
Red wine vinegar
Cider vinegar
Soft brown sugar
Tomato passata
Caster sugar
Runny honey
Caraway seeds
Bicarbonate of soda
Baking powder
Whole nutmeg
Cayenne pepper
Vanilla essence
Tomato puree

About Amanda Wragg

Amanda Wragg is a freelance food and feature writer, born in Derbyshire and now based near Hebden Bridge on the Pennines. She writes for the Yorkshire Post, Alastair Sawday, Square Meal and the AA. She sits on several judging panels for regional and national food & drink awards, inspects and writes for a well-known restaurant review publication and co-writes a website dedicated to good places to eat and stay in Yorkshire, www.squidbeak.co.uk

About Joan Ransley

Joan Ransley is a food photojournalist based in Ilkley, West Yorkshire. She works for local and national publications including The Yorkshire Post, Yorkshire Life, Derbyshire Life, The University of Leeds, The Guardian and the online Travel Magazine – Food Tripper. Joan is a member of the Guild of Food Writers. www.joanransley.co.uk